The Taborist

2014 Poetry Collection

by

Eric Nixon

Cover image and design by Eric Nixon.

ISBN-13: 978-0692424575
ISBN-10: 0692424571
BISAC: Poetry / American / General

Published by Double Yolk Press in Portland, Oregon.
EricNixonAuthor@gmail.com
EricNixon.net

DEDICATION

This collection is dedicated to Ron & Robyn Chapin. I hugely appreciate your encouragement and support!

Thank you!

AUTHOR'S FOREWARD

2014 was a very different year, which resulted in a different poetry collection than I had expected. 2014 was the first full year I lived in Portland, Oregon. It was also the year I returned to my long-time career of being a hotel manager; the most important aspect of which meant that I no longer had the luxury of nearly unlimited time to write about whatever whim crossed my path, like I enjoyed in 2013 with my collection, *The Entire Universe*. With briefer windows of time to write, I would sometimes go entire months without putting my fingers to a keyboard for the sake of poetry or expression. Here and there I would get back into it, but it wasn't until the end of the year I made a concerted effort to make up for a "dry" poetry year.

You'll no doubt ask, "What is a 'taborist'?" Honestly, I don't know. I live near an extinct volcano core named Mount Tabor. I see the trees from it peek out over the rooftops of my neighbor's houses when I walk the dogs. Sometimes, when I want some exercise, I'll huff it up the mile and a half of gradually steepening terrain that separates my house with what I call the 1st Level of the mountain. I guess a Taborist is a person who spends a lot of time on, or near, Mount Tabor. By that definition would I call myself a taborist? No. The most time I spent on the mountain in one day was last August when they had the PDX Adult Soapbox Derby and I spent four hours at the finish line watching the fun and funny vehicles zip (or limp) past. Still though, I think that people have a tendency to personify and identify with prominent geological landmarks of their immediate home area. When I grew up in Dalton, Massachusetts, I would look out my bedroom window at the layers upon layers of gently rolling hills and feel a special comfort from them; as if they were "hugging" me in. Here and now, in my current neighborhood in Portland, Oregon, the big thing I see from my house is the backdrop that Mount Tabor provides. Hence, *The Taborist.*

Enjoy,
Eric

TABLE OF CONTENTS

Antiquated Format

A Glance With Meaning
Empty Walls

December – 21
Searching For The 31st
From The Stranger You
The Kinetic Crew
Tabor Rainbow
Innocent
We Can Consumer Our Way Out Of This
Where Your Past Sleeps Soundly
The Next Day
Cross-Contamination
Porch Party
Creativity
Betelgeusing Toward Tabor
Clumsy Superhero
Defeated And Reheated
Between November And Now
Like Cordwood
Sidestepping Crow
Energy
Before Handwriting Fell
A Field Day
Every Second
Looking Back On This Year

2014 total: 112

JANUARY

Lessened

January first
Lights diminished
Goodwill lessened
Spirit redacted
Christmas removed
Season finished
All of it is
Over and done

> January 1, 2014
> Portland, Oregon

The neighbors have been taking down Christmas. It's pretty much over and done with.

The Amber Of Doubt

The hope of the day and the freshly born year
Is being encased in the amber of doubt
With every passing minute
As the negatron vacuum
Sweeps in and sucks up
The positrons
As quickly as they are generated
Leaving a vacuum in its place

January 1, 2014
Portland, Oregon

Delayed Adherent

Hold me off and make me wait
Giving a red light
To the speeding racers
So close to the finish line
Stuck inside, nowhere to go
Delayed, adherent to the whims
Of the one with the smirk
Whose hand is on the trigger
Controlling things from above

January 4, 2014
Portland, Oregon

Lines In The Sky

Lines in the sky
Running everywhere
Connecting everything
Highly visible but
Completely invisible
To normal people
On their normal routines
But ever present
And always in the way
Cutting, slicing, ruining
The lines of sight
Barging their way in
Making their presence known
Spoiling perfect scenes
For photographers like me

January 4, 2014
Portland, Oregon

Wow, there are a crap-ton of very tall telephone poles strung up with a dizzying number of power lines in Portland.

Bestow The Craved Burdens

Affix the lofty position,
Adorn me with the title,
Click the nametag in place,
Bestow the craved burdens,
And watch the confident me
Radiantly shine through
Stepping into the role
After a five-year break,
Amazingly to the day,
As if only a day had passed
And watch me go
Just like I always did
Just like I always will

January 16, 2014
Portland, Oregon

After a five-year absence (to the day!) I resume my career as a
hotelier.

Silver Smudge Above

Silver smudge up above
Behind the clouds
Muted, subdued,
But giving enough light
Shining through
Nature's cumulus curtain
To set the filtered mood
Upon those down below

January 16, 2014
Portland, Oregon

I'm really enjoying the super-foggy nights we've been having lately.

The Number Taker

Waiting in a place completely reliant
On the red "Take A Number" dispenser
When in walks an attituded girl
Who clearly gives no fucks
As she looked at the number on the wall,
Looked at the number she had just received,
Popped open the clam-like dispenser
Yanking out arm-lengths of numbers
One, two, three, four,
Losing count as she is focused on one thing.
The desk, unbeknownst, called the next number
And someone rose only to be cut off
By the girl, blameless in her mind,
A strand of numbers snaking around her feet
Saying, "I've got it! That's my number!"
Only to be betrayed by the starting letter
Devised by the red number dispenser company
For just such an occasion
As if they had previously encountered
Or somehow psychically predicted
This very same situation
And created a clever solution
To thwart her devious intentions

January 17, 2014
Portland, Oregon

I could not believe what I was seeing when this happened. It was
equally brilliant and crazy-shitty all at once. She was found out and
thrown out, of course.

Foot-Step, Foot-Step

A long walk
Longer thinking
Foot-step, foot-step
Absorbing everything
Taking in my surroundings
The uneven sidewalk squares
Each and every house I pass by
The lights strung up just because
Homes adorned with distinct personality
Reflecting my innermost being
While my mind delves deeply
Thinking of new possibilities
A future me unrecognized
Just mere weeks before
Foot-step, foot-step
Thinking longer
On a long walk

January 17, 2014
Portland, Oregon

I've been walking a lot since moving to Portland. It's been great exercise and has been giving me a time to think about my present and focus on my future.

Past My Bedtime

The corner-screen clock
Tries to tell me it's late
And past my bedtime
But the inside me
Is tending to disagree
As my body presses on
Fueled with a deep well
Of boundless creativity

> January 17, 2014
> Portland, Oregon

That being said, I think I might actually go to bed.

Exhibitionist City

It's difficult to watch where I'm going
When nearly every house's window
It wide open and freely broadcasting
The contents of the lives inside
It's as if there's no such thing
As curtains here in exhibitionist city
Where everyone is really trying
To be as open and accessible
As possible while not caring
What us by-passers might see

>   January 18, 2014
>   Portland, Oregon

Seriously, probably 90% of all the houses I walk by have open, un-curtained windows. I'm not used to this. People in New England are not this open and showy.

In The Flooded Sky

Walking along, enjoying the night
Looking up, catching my eye
Moving slightly, my periphery tilts
Forefronting the gently sliding dot
Seeing there, in the flooded sky
Gliding light, a discernable satellite
Something I thought I'd never know
Living here, in the middle of a city

January 18, 2014
Portland, Oregon

When I lived in rural Vermont, I saw satellites pass by overhead several times a week. It seemed that, if it was clear, and I looked up, I'd most likely see a satellite. Here, there is so much light pollution flooding out the heavens, I can only see the brightest of stars; which is why I was surprised to see one gliding across the sky.

Formless

An astounding heap
A piled-high collection
Comprised of thoughts,
Ramblings, and a million awkward moments
The ones that would take far too long to explain
And compound the embarrassment,
Along with seemingly random bits
Which are connected in a convoluted way
Making perfect sense to my synapses
All of which run through my mind
Faster than I can catch
Which is why the dam is firmly shut –
I don't open my mouth
For fear that it would all spill out
Like a formless disjointed jumble
Blasting forth at the speed of light
Instantly alienating those around me
Who can't, or can't be bothered,
To connect the dots
Or keep up

        January 18, 2014
        Portland, Oregon

There was no pre-planning with this. I just wrote.

Recapture The Bygone (What Can Never Be Held Again)

Live a life
So full
So rich
So packed with living
And enjoying
There's no room or time
For nostalgia
Which will pause the present,
Dampen your current positivity,
And direct your precious energy
Back, behind you, to the past
And, at the very least,
Slowing you down
And, at the most,
Stopping you completely
And reversing direction
In a futile attempt
To recapture the bygone
And cling to what can never be held again

So yeah, don't do that.
Keep moving
Keep growing
Keep expanding
Keep becoming
What you were meant to be
Not what you once were

                    January 23, 2014
                    Portland, Oregon

I wrote the first seven lines the other night while on a walk and just
finished it up.

The Mask Of Another

Sometimes the mask
Of another
Fits much better
Than the one
That won't come off

January 23, 2014
Portland, Oregon

Every couple of nights, I pop onto my Emily Dickinson, Superhero Twitter account (@EmilyDSuperhero) and reply to people who Tweet about Emily. I really enjoy it and love trying to get into her head and reply to them as if it really were her. I even feel myself take personal offense when some high-schooler says something like, "Emily Dickinson is a bitch."

Like A Whisper Skin

Seconds or hours
Neither of us knows
The only thing certain
Is the inner darkness
Of eyes firmly shut
Enhancing the sensing
Instinctively responding
Toes tightening
Flexing and curling
Sharp intakes of breath
Caused by something
So hinted and light
Creating longing
Like a whisper skin
Moving down
Tracing along
Leaving shivering
Stretching muscles
Trailing behind
In its nuanced wake

January 24, 2014
Portland, Oregon

I was listening to Cat Power's "3,6,9" in the car tonight and
thought she said, "whisper skin" at one point. I later looked up the
lyrics to the song and I was totally wrong but liked the imagery it
conjured.

A Winterish Comparison Of Two Coasts

Here:
The world is perfect
Bright light warmth
Radiating down
A light jacket worn
To ward off the light wind

There:
The world is hushed
Bright white snow
Falling down
A heavy jacket worn
To hold off the cold wind

January 25, 2014
Portland, Oregon

Portland Oregon versus Great Barrington, Massachusetts. Our friend Alana Chernila posted a photo on her Instagram with the caption, "The world is hushed." I know exactly what she means and that feeling inspired this.

Ample

Everything
About me,
And I do,
In every way
Is ample;
Larger than life
Bigger than needed
From goals
To happiness
Moving through
These times
In a greater way

January 25, 2014
Portland, Oregon

Pizza Penance

If I want something bad for me
Let's say, a pizza
I don't hop in the car
To drive the 1.1 miles
I make myself walk it
To serve a pizza penance
As a way to walk off
The anticipatory calories
In advance of the eating
No matter the weather
No matter my desires;
If I want it, I walk it

> January 27, 2014
> Portland, Oregon

This has served as a great system. I've been steadily losing weight every week.

FEBRUARY

Tabor Sunrise

The promise of every new morning
Starts with the Tabor sunrise
At first hiding and concealing
The gentle morning-soft light
Until the hill is radiating
Glowing its yellow-rayed crown
Before finally launching it arcward
Through the breaking clouds
Sailing across the blue bowl
Freely giving it
To the remaining day
Until it's caught and snuffed out
By the park-topped Council Crest
Not before saying thank you
And lavishing its light
Upon the morning giver

February 1, 2014
Portland, Oregon

I was pretty impressed by the nice light this morning while
walking the dogs.

Back In The Game

Overjoyed at the news
Of someone telling me to do
Something everyone else
Takes for granted
Every Monday through Friday
And I will be there
The required hours
Plus as many as it takes
Wearing an oversized smile
Thankful to be back in the game

February 5, 2014
Portland, Oregon

Today, I was hired back as a manager with the GIANT HOTEL
COMPANY I previously worked at for nine years.

Beyond The Time

Plans made beyond the time
When thoughts and actions freely
Collide and conspire unreservedly
Making the soon-to-be present
Something bright and wonderfully
Attractive giving something deservedly
Wonderful to strive for and achieve

February 5, 2014
Portland, Oregon

A City That Can't Clean Up

Snow
Where it doesn't belong
Continues to fall
Covering, deepening
Making a mess of things
In a city that can't clean up

>   February 7, 2014
>   Portland, Oregon

There's maybe three inches on the ground and more falling. I know snow only falls here once every couple of years, but I assumed the city would have had a better plan in place instead of, "Wait for it to melt."

Press On The Brakes

The intensity of the rain
That deluged the day today
Obscuring the road I drove on
Causing the caution
To press on the brakes
Was inversely proportional
To the emotions I feel
When I think of the bond
I'm legally obligated to have
Making my path and my way
As crystal clear as the absent air
I try to breathe in this house

February 15, 2014
Portland, Oregon

There was a crazy-intense rainstorm this afternoon, which is weird
because from what I've read the rain pretty much only falls in a
gentle drizzle here.

Displayed Taborward

After the intense falling
Of the inescapable rain
The sky lightened
And the clouds parted
Allowing the day's
Brightly-edged puffy ceiling
To have their way
With the sky above
Contrasting and aweing
Catching and impressing
Those who choose to see
The projected brilliance
Of the dulled rainbow
Displayed Taborward

February 15, 2014
Portland, Oregon

Pressure Applied

Pressure applied
From a place
I have no attachment to
From a person
I care nothing about
Demanding that I
Buy BUY *BUY!*
Right now
Treating me like a school kid
That's deeply in trouble
Forgetting completely
That I have a choice
With whom I spend my money
So I left
Because I refused to be
Bossed, bullied, and sullied
By his negatively demanding attitude

February 22, 2014
Portland, Oregon

I went to look at and test drive a Fiat because I'm looking to buy one soon. The sales guy was nice and fine, but he had his "service manager" come in who was a total dick to me. I was actually taken aback by how awful this guy acted towards me. No smiles, all demands, extremely pressure-y and said that the information my long-time, very trusted insurance company told me was nothing but lies. Whatever. See if I buy a car from you.

A Minty Breeze

In the extreme latitudes
Look up to catch sight
Of a minty breeze rippled
With occasional raspberry
Silently winding above
Like an ethereal ballet
Ribboning and snaking
In time to The Magnetic Fields
Surrounding and enveloping us all

February 22, 2014
Portland, Oregon

Tonight Kari asked how I would describe something she thought was indescribable to a blind person: the northern lights. After a few seconds, I said, "a minty breeze."

Lessening The Layers

Lessening the layers
Thinning down the coats
As spring raises the numbers
Of that invisible backdrop
Staging the unfolding scene

> February 26, 2014
> Portland, Oregon

It was almost 60 today and the flowers are just barely starting to bloom.

March

The Taborist

MARCH

The Murder

The murder of crows
Numbered a hefty slaughter
Darkly raving their brash calls
And passed judgment on me
Passing on by below

>   March 1, 2014
>   Portland, Oregon

The other day there was maybe 50 crows hanging out in a tree across the street. I was walking the dogs and they apparently had a lot to say about it.

Mahogany Dreams

Mahogany dreams
Framed in teak
Particleboard reality
Edged with pine

March 28, 2014
Portland, Oregon

I was looking at my poetry notes in my phone and saw the first line sitting there by itself and all of a sudden had the inspiration to quick this one out.

Antiquated Format

Big in the hand
Bulky with its appearance
Incomprehensible in the brain
That this antiquated format
Used to be a normal part
Of a normal life
Not all that long ago

March 31, 2014
Portland, Oregon

When I look at a cassette player, or even a cassette, this is what runs through my head. 90 minutes of music on a piece of magnetic tape inside a plastic case is the same size as my (now old) iPod which contains 30,000 songs.

APRIL

Through The Consciousness Catching

Some of the more abstract moments
That percolate and permeate
Through the consciousness catching
Are the ones worth hugging, knowing,
And getting in depth with
For those are the thoughts
Dressed in originality
Dapper and ready
For lifetime of reflection
Or, at the very least,
A fun night out on the town

April 20, 2014
Portland, Oregon

Property Lines

Property lines
Are not decided by surveyors
But instead
By mowers

April 20, 2014
Portland, Oregon

A sure-fire way to know where one property ends and another begins is to look for the line that separates the shaggy grass from the tidy.

Your Next Action

Your next action
Should be dictated
By the following question:
Have you left your mark
Firmly and permanently
Upon the day?
When the night shrouds
Life in the present
Are you confident
That your name and deeds
Will survive the temporary cell
That houses the undying you?

If not, keep at it.

> April 20, 2014
> Portland, Oregon

Achieve the greatness you were meant to attain.

Tabor's Growing Crown

Above the apexed eaves
Between the chimneys
Haloed by the morning rays
Juts the barbed jeweled tops
Of Tabor's growing crown
Green sharply silhouetted
By the living warming yellow
Giving me everything I need
As the right way to be introduced
To the new day just beginning

April 20, 2014
Portland, Oregon

While walking the dogs a week or so ago, I looked back and saw the radiating light blasting through the trees of Mount Tabor. It was glorious.

The Persistent Whisper

The persistent whisper
Of the deeply inner me
Expressing my needs
Clearer than clearly
Wanting what I can't give
Demanding acquiescence
Which I cannot consent to
Not at the moment
Not right now
But maybe someday
Who knows
Least of all, me

April 20, 2014
Portland, Oregon

The voice is not mine, but it is within me.

The Comforting Shudder

My life is filled with awe and wonder
As I see the world in a whole new light
Traits I am discovering with each footfall
As the puzzle pieces click firmly into place
With each realization that hits me
Like an epiphanal punch in the gut
Accompanied with the comforting shudder
Of reassurance, of knowing, of confidence
That where I am
What I am doing
And where I am heading
Is perfectly in line and aligned
With where I need to be

> April 20, 2014
> Portland, Oregon

My real-life superpower is being in the exactly right place at the right time.

Mount Hood Is Trying To Kill Me

Mount Hood is trying to kill me
With its apexed-steeped beauty
The toothy triangle sitting large
Way over there to my distant left
As I drive over the bridge linking
Washington to Oregon distracting
Pulling my attention off the road
Appreciating the folds and shadows
The early evening setting sun casts
And splashes across the glaciers
With its peachy-pink-hued glow
Illuminating details…
MMMMMMMMRRRRRRRRR!
Blaring horn yanking me back
Overcorrecting to a near-miss
Amid evasive maneuvers
On the part of those more aware
More horns blaring, drowning out
My meek apologies interspersed
And seeded with profanities
Punctuating each almost-collision
Along with hearty brake-squealing
Until it evened out after a barrage
Of finger-flipping and curses
Aimed squarely at my poor car
An innocent intermediary
Fully in control of my soul
Which was caught by the lure
Of that devious strato-volcano
Fully intent on one day seeing me
Flip over the edge of the bridge
Falling hundreds of screaming feet

Into the cold Columbia death below

April 28, 2014
Portland, Oregon

Every. Single. Time. I see Mount Hood I am completely entranced by its hugeness and its beauty. This makes it difficult to drive over the I-205 bridge over the Columbia River on my way home every night because, damn, it's so beautiful I can't help but to stare.

MAY

The Sometimes Side Of Me

A grittiness favored
For the abrasive nature
Scrubbing off the day
While the chaotic nature
Provides the sounding antithesis
To the clean-cut outwardness
And the heavy layered overcoat;
A sonic armor worn
Around my car
And myself
Expressing the sometimes side of me

May 10, 2014
Portland, Oregon

Tonight, while doing some work on the computer, I put on my "Gritty" playlist on iTunes with music from bands like The Ravonettes, An Horse, The Pinehurst Kids, and Rainer Maria, popped open my Line Ideas document, and wrote this.

Catch The Light

Just in time to catch the light
That is as fleeting as youth
The perfect moment
That lasts no longer
And is quickly captured
By the mind and the memory
And becomes a replayed photo
That lasts forever past
The last synapse sparked
By earthly intention

> May 31, 2014
> Portland, Oregon

Watching, and appreciating, the late-night setting sunlight
perfectly illuminating the beauty of my surroundings.

Stick Figure Family

Stick figure family prominently displayed
In the back window of the family minivan
With one obvious and glaring exception:
One of the two big stick figures
Had been deliberately scraped off
I assume by the remaining stick figure
The one parent left owning the van
And controlling custody of the kids
Trying to remove the sticky memory
Of the other that's no longer in the picture
Leaving the casual observer
Left to awkward speculation

May 31, 2014
Portland, Oregon

Gee whiz, if you're going to scrape your ex's stick figure sticker
off your car, at least move the kids over so it doesn't look as
obvious.

Linked Beyond

A suitable sound
Entering my ears
From the speakers
Linked beyond
Just mere liking
From and to
Something deeper
A welcome me
That I want to see
Completed
In such a way
That hasn't been
Tried, attempted, done
Before

May 31, 2014
Portland, Oregon

Move A Little Faster

Waiting for the past to catch up
To the accelerated nature
That I've become in the ensuing years
But time is running out
For me to be sitting here
Doing nothing but waiting
So onward I must move
Forever and always
And if I start on before they've caught up
Well, that just means
They need to move a little faster

May 31, 2014
Portland, Oregon

May

AUGUST

What Happened To June And July?

What happened to June and July?
I blinked and summer slipped by

August 9, 2014
Portland, Oregon

Between work during the day, and working on editing *2492* at
night, the past few months have been oddly poetry-free. At least
when I was writing *Emily Dickinson, Superhero*, I was spending
time at least thinking about poetry which, in turn, compelled me to
write some. Not so with an action-based sci-fi novel. Anyway, I
love this poem because it's crazy short, double-rhymey, and
beautifully succinct.

An Upright Wrench

An upright wrench
Holding open a window
Probably not the ideal way
To prop it such a short length
But it's the one that works
The way it needs to for them

> August 9, 2014
> Portland, Oregon

I was walking home from the library and looked up to a nearby house and saw a second story window being propped open with a wrench. Out of all the things to open a window with, that was the best choice?

Their Thirst Exposed

Each and every Sunday evening
Under the protective shroud of night
The neighbors sneak out to the curb,
Drop their shame, and hustle back in
Hoping their mission was completed unseen

Walking the dogs the next morning
The fresh sun's light illuminates
Their recycling bins and all at once
The extent of their thirst is exposed
And we all learn a lot more about one another

August 9, 2014
Portland, Oregon

Deflating Knowing

Recently I came face to face
With the essential, inward, eternal me
Where I was to learn my life's purpose
And the resulting takeaway
Has rendered me unsettled
And slightly disappointed
After finding out that I'm on the right track
And to keep up the good work
When I was hoping to learn
Something new, exciting, and Earth-shattering
When I was expecting to get a list
Of things I needed to change right away
Instead of being told I am where I need to be
Which I guess is a good thing
Actually, a great thing
But still, it's a little deflating knowing
That, as usual, the dependable me
Is at the right place at the right time,
Right where I should be

> August 9, 2014
> Portland, Oregon

Intended Consequence

The brightly colorful ad in the magazine
Promises complete relief from what ails you
Until you turn the page and find four more pages
Packed with words in a tiny, hard-to-read font
Full of information they don't really want you to read
But they are governmentally compelled to print
Listing all of the terrible and horrible side-effects
That taking their doctor-prescribed product
Can cause its unwitting users
Who can't be bothered to read beyond
The large-type boastful headline
But not to worry because they happen to have
More pills to deal with those issues as well
Leading to their intended consequence
Of a pill tornado swirling down every throat
In every city, in every state, in every country

August 9, 2014
Portland, Oregon

Seeing drug ads makes me sick. (Ha!)

A Worthwhile Investment

Any time spent contemplating
Who we are, why we're here,
What is our essential being,
And what lies beyond the present
Is a worthwhile investment
For the eternal knowledge
Which we find worth seeking

August 9, 2014
Portland, Oregon

The super-important stuff doesn't pay at all, yet rewards us with riches beyond measure.

My Mind Is Clothed With A Vividness

While I am crowded with an endless
Experience beyond my years
My mind is clothed with a vividness,
A youth that subvents my age
Which is detached from my wrinkles
By a creatively-sourced wellspring
Of artistically appreciated newness

August 9, 2014
Portland, Oregon

That's "subvents" not "subverts." Think of a geological subduction zone where one layer of the crust is pushed under another. That's probably not the exact right thing, but the vague concept of it was in my mind as I wrote it.

Yards Should Not Be Measured

Yards should not be measured
By square footage
Or deemed worthy
By the cut and color of the grass

Other factors need to be considered
Like how it's used
The hours of joy
And the happiness the space provides

August 17, 2014
Portland, Oregon

I feel bad for people who only care for how "perfect" their yards look but otherwise never lay a foot on them.

The Spill In The Corner

The spill in the corner
Seeping, spreading
Between the neighbor's roof
And the distant Tabor-top trees
Diffusing rose, up and outward
Staining the puffy layer
Painting the ceiling
For such a short time
Paving the way for the morning
Giving a great start
For us lucky witnesses
Before the sun awoke
Rising, changing the angle
And erasing the work it had done
On the other side of the horizon

August 17, 2014
Portland, Oregon

Zoe, the cat, meowed her head off and woke me up early. After I stumbled into the kitchen and fed her, I stood in awe at how amazing the sunrise looked as it painted the clouds a magnificent rose color. Thanks, Zoe.

The Beautiful Conclusion

Fearing death is a wasted endeavor
One we spend all too much time on.
It's something we've done
Countless times before
And will continue to do
Countless times again.
The more energy spent
Worrying and stressing
About the finality of life
Is energy squandered
On something you can't control
Instead of spending it living
And making the most
Of the moment you're in now.
So, when faced with finality
Just close your eyes and enjoy
The beautiful conclusion…

You'll be back soon enough

August 17, 2014
Portland, Oregon

Disco Yappers

Happy double-long dogs
Trit-trotting along the sidewalk
Tails a-wagging,
Nails a-click-clacking
Side-by-side into the night
Their light-up collars
Drawing attention
And showing the way
Until they come across
A nearby neighbor
Who sees them, laughs,
And calls the boys
"Disco yappers."
Unknowing and undeterred
They continued along their walk
Never knowing their new titles
And honestly, probably
Wouldn't even care if they knew

August 17, 2014
Portland, Oregon

This happened the other night.

I Am The Spark

I am the spark
The sunbeam
The daylight
That gets others going
The inspiration
The motivation
That keeps people creating
The fueller of dreams
The speed limitless sign
On the highway of creativity
I am the hidden
And the heard
I am the written
And the observed
It is my job to do all of these
So you can do yours

> August 17, 2014
> Portland, Oregon

I wrote most of this last October, right after we moved to Portland. I think I was writing about how I am the main motivator and source of inspiration for Kari who, in turn, inspires tens of thousands of others with her work.

Only Four Slices

Only four slices
Are needed
With a sharp knife.
Entry is easy:
Pierce the binder layer,
Slide across,
Opposite to your dexterousness;
Once slice on a short side,
Once slice the long way
From end to end,
Followed by a quick succession
Of the remaining short side
Now divided into two halves,
Flip the flaps skyward
And entry has been achieved

August 17, 2014
Portland, Oregon

This was another one I wrote in October right after we moved to Portland and was unpacking all of the moving boxes. I tidied it up and here it is.

Unfettered Access

Free connection
Just sitting there
All wide open
No pause
No questions
No hesitation
Permitting all
Each and every
Unfettered access
So casually
So blasé
So nonchalantly
Like it was nothing
Nothing at all

August 18, 2014
Portland, Oregon

Another poem I mostly wrote when I first moved to Portland. This is about the free Wi-Fi at the café a block away that tided us over until our home Internet connection was hooked up.

A Full Meal Of Stars

In Vermont the night sky
Was a full meal of stars,
Satellites, and dreams
Previously unknown
To my Massachusetts eyes.

While visiting Sedona,
I was bursting stuffed
From the overfull plate
Of the Milky Way
Edge-on and pouring
Its previously unfathomable
Nearly endless buffet
Into my hungry appreciation.

Portland, Oregon, however,
Has a sky comprised solely
Of the brightest scraps…
And nothing else,
Leaving me so very hungry.

> August 18, 2014
> Portland, Oregon

Sometime, I need to get out to the coast to see the stars above the Pacific at night. When that happens, I'll write a rebuttal.

Also, in my notes I had originally wrote after, "…and nothing else," "Much like the CD selection at any big box store." Funny and true, but it didn't quite fit.

Equally Funny And Scary

It's equally funny and scary
To watch the superstitious
And the just plain ignorant
Get their collective panties
In a brain-crushing twist
As "reddish" becomes "blood red"
And a simple shadow
Passing in front of the moon
Is equated with the end of the world
In this modern day and age

August 23, 2014
Portland, Oregon

Written a few months ago when there was an eclipse and groups of derpy people were filling the Internet and the news with "OMG! We're all going to die! It's the end of the world!"

We're all still here.

The Cranberry Bog

An important location to my younger self
When we'd venture an hour west
To go shopping in upstate New York
And we'd stop for lunch
At The Cranberry Bog
The type of restaurant
That's since been lost to time
Independent and appealing
To an older generation
Before it was beaten down
By the chains and the era
But back then it was something
That deeply impressed
The eight-year-old me
The mood, the feeling, the food,
And the free matchboxes
With the logo of the cute whale
Splashing out of the water
Which, I know, has nothing
To do with cranberry bogs
But it still made the memory.
Even though the ensuing years
Made me forget about the place,
That closed a decade and a half later
Unbeknownst to the millennial self,
Until each move when I'd uncover
A bag of old matchbooks I'd saved
From when I was a kid who cared
About such silly trivial things,
Seeing the tiny cardboard box
With the dry sticks rattling around
Inside its coffin-like souvenir
I would be forced to think about the Bog
The times spent there with my family
The times that can never be recovered
Or ever lived the same way again
When the matches are gone

So will be the reminder
And the memories will follow
Fading across decades
With nothing to bring them back

August 23, 2014
Portland, Oregon

There were a bunch of restaurants like this we went to that would seem like out-of-time relics now. All I have left to remind me are a few matchboxes that are 30-years old, and every year a few more get used up and thrown out. Soon, there will be nothing left of them.

Racing Down Tabor

The sun beating down
The car bearing down
Quickly racing down
The extinct volcano core
Each trying to out-do one another
In looks, in hustle, in quirkiness
Some were built just for speed
Others were designed for smiles
Some blasted across the finish
Others were pushed to the line
No matter the reason, watching
The adult soapbox derby cars
Racing down Tabor
Was a great way to spend the day

August 23, 2014
Portland, Oregon

This was a lot of fun.

Portland Is An Island

Portland is an island
In the middle of the sea
Surrounded by
Gently lapping hills
And fields so empty
Miles with nothing
Strung loosely together
Hours until something
Surfaces and rises
To catch my interest
And hold it long enough
To attempt a landing
So, for the time being
Apart from the occasional
Exploratory forays to see
All there is to experience
I'm content to stay here
Safely ensconced
Within the walls
Of my chosen land

August 30, 2014
Portland, Oregon

Maybe I'm heading in the wrong direction when I leave the city to explore, but it seems like there's a whole lot of nothing within a three-hour ring outside of Portland. It's definitely not like New England where I could visit six states and so many interesting places within three hours of home. In the future, I think I need to do more research before I go out. Neat things could be out there, I just might not know about them.

Misty Wet Step

Stepping outside the shop
Walking across my city
Feeling the faint traces
Stepping the misty wet step
Enjoying the welcomed coolness
Airing the traces of moisture
Like a supermarket produce aisle
Fractioning so much lighter
Where none of it is minded
And all of it is welcomed
Clouding out the beating sun
Fittingly ending this hot summer
On Labor Day weekend
Previewing an easy glimpse
Of the winter yet to come

August 30, 2014
Portland, Oregon

The weather was so nice walking to and from the barbershop
today.

Living Expectantly

I know the beginning
I know the now
I know the ending
I happen to know how
Things will turn out
But what I don't know
Is the space between
Here and there,
This and that,
Present and final future
So I'll just make it up
As I venture along
And watch as everything
Lines up accordingly;
In the meantime I'll be
Smiling happily as I'm
Living expectantly

        August 30, 2014
        Portland, Oregon

SEPTEMBER

Back For The Cap

A hipstery-looking man
Wearing a trucker hat
Over chunky glasses
Perfectly perched above
An overly bushy moustache
With a microbrewed six-pack
In-hand walking down the street
Doubletaked, paused, and stopped
When he saw my recycling bin
Looking past the empty peanut butter jar
His eyes locked on the empty bottle
Of Ommegang Three Philosophers
A Belgian-style quadruple ale
Infused with a topping of cherries
Brewed in Cooperstown, New York
The recognition clicked deeply
As he looked to my kitchen window
And tipped his hat in reverence
And appreciation as he turned
And went back for the cap
Which he popped off
And dropped in his pocket
As he went along his way
With an extra pep in his step

> September 21, 2014
> Portland, Oregon

This actually happened. It's nice to be appreciated for the quality of beer I drink.

The Fixed Life

The fixed life
Our parents expected
A fixed job
Married with a family
In a fixed address
Never moving
Only knowing
The town
The people
The things
There and nowhere else
And the immediate area
But
When life
When companies
Choose the easier
The cheaper path
Things change
Beyond what is known
Beyond what is expected
Beyond the comprehension
Instilled within their youthful selves
And allowances must be made
The kind that change lives
The kind that break families
And skew them, fling them
Off in a different direction
Than what was known
Than what was expected
The recovery from which
Takes years

September 21, 2014
Portland, Oregon

I sometimes think of the type of life my parents expected to have and what actually happened framed with the perspective of General Electric and their decision to close down everything in Pittsfield, Massachusetts.

September

The Taborist

OCTOBER

More

The hungriest person
Can assuage and satiate
Their gluttonest desires
With an overstuffed meal
Because there is something,
A mechanism in place,
To prevent the wholesale gorging,
The unlimited devouring,
Of everything in sight

According to the law
Companies are people
With one specific difference:
Their hunger knows no limits.
They only know one word:
More.
More revenue.
More money.
Raise prices.
Cut services.
Be leaner, more profitable.
Deliver more
To the bottom line.
More.

Never mind it's 24% more
Than just two years before
No time to celebrate.
Do it
Never mind it's statistically impossible
To continue this pace
For more than a year or two
Do it
Do it or lose
Your job
Your colleagues
Your career

Your way of life
The insatiable maw
Knows nothing
But the singular concept
Of more.
Do more with less.
Double up on that workload.
Do the jobs of five people.
Triple those projections,
And do more.
More
More

More.

October 18, 2014
Portland, Oregon

That maw will never be satisfied with anything less.

Photographs

Photographs
Hold memories
Hold energy
Hold power over us
When we need it
Just a glance
And we are taken back
To a different time
With the person
Emotions flood and fill us
As we remember
How things once were
And we are comforted
As we face uncertainty
When times are changing
But, much like a key,
Specific photographs
Will unlock the heart
Of those they are meant for
If seen by a stranger
Chances are slim
Any feelings will arise
The same goes for
Photographs
Which are kept
Hidden away
In books, boxes,
Or hard drives
Where they are unable
To do their job

October 26, 2014
Portland, Oregon

Everything has energy. It just depends on how much we choose to assign to something.

Illuminating

Those people who say,
"Look at the light,"
Are doing a great disservice
And really only want
To keep you in the dark.
Don't look at the light;
You'll be blinded.
Instead look to see
What the light
Is illuminating.
Just as you wouldn't look
Directly at the Sun
But would focus instead
On what the Sun is showing.

          October 26, 2014
          Portland, Oregon

I don't know about you, but I'd rather not be blinded so I can fully appreciate what this world has to offer.

Welcome Change

Some years the leaves fall down
And I am sad to see the season go
As the colors carpet the region
And clothes on the people layer up

This year, however, feels different
I am actually looking forward to it
Fully embracing the cold months
And the welcome change it brings

October 26, 2014
Portland, Oregon

I am ready.

When I Cast My Line

I am thankful
For the unending ocean
Of creativity
That flows in my head
The depth of which
Is seemingly endless
The breadth of which
Knows no bounds
The substance of which
Is solidly reliable
It may ebb from time to time
But I know beyond a doubt
Of the dependability
I will experience
When I cast my line
And find, without fail,
Each and every time
I will reel in something good

October 26, 2014
Portland, Oregon

I'm not being braggy, just thankful.

This Is Existence

This is existence
Right now
This very moment
And no other
Pause
And reflect
On your surroundings
And your place among it
Keeping in mind
To record every detail
No matter how small
And insignificant
Because in the end
It all matters
It's all there for a reason
Things to remind you
Lessons to work on
Fences to mend
Futures to build
Pause again
And separate
The past
And the future
From all thought
Strain them right out
Like the pulp
From your orange juice
And toss it aside
Because it doesn't matter
None of it matters
The past is done
And can't be changed
The future hasn't happened
And can be re-arranged
Focus on right now
This moment
And nothing else

Don't just see your surroundings
But experience them
Note every infinitesimal detail
Feel why it's there
Right now
In your path
And grow
From knowing
And living
The past will try
To assert itself
And creep deep
Into your periphery
In order to distract
And pull you back
To a previous time
DON'T LET IT
Because if you do
You'll be wasting
Your present
Digging into the deepening
Repeating groove
That distorts to your ideals
And changes slightly
With each ensuing spin
Playing Telephone
With your younger self
While Photoshopping
And brightening
The edges
To something softer
To something better
More suited to replay
Than what actually happened
So resist the need to replay
And focus your senses
On just and only today
Don't just see
But smell the moment

Breathe deeply
Take it all in
Let the season,
Your surroundings,
The fragrant,
The pungent,
The sounds,
The feelings,
Let it all in
And blend
Bookmarking a reminder
Of this very moment
Somewhere within your mind
Starting now
And staying with you
For all time

October 26, 2014
Portland, Oregon

Lumperbum

Every day, a new name
For the waggeriffic dog
Who defies description
On a seemingly daily basis
Yesterday it was the simple:
Dr. Professor Mr. Wag Wag
Today, the odd: Lumperbum
Tomorrow? I have no idea
But you can be assured
It'll be something new

October 26, 2014
Portland, Oregon

A weird one! I called Baxter, "Lumperbum," the other day for no real reason. As I started to write, the lines seemed to be the same length, and then grow slightly. I honestly was a lot more focused on the shape of the poem than the contents within it.

Assurance

I've seen a glimpse of my future
A momentary snippet of a scene
Lasting just a second
But that was enough
To feel the emotions
To know how everything turns out
So I can now live with assurance
And free my mind of any worry

October 26, 2014
Portland, Oregon

This past summer I saw a hypnotherapist and I did a Life Between Lives session. To be free of fear and to know the reasons behind everything (who I am, why I'm here, what my purpose is, etc) has been the most freeing thing I have ever experienced. While under, I cheated slightly and looked ahead. I ended up seeing a momentary flash of my future self and it was hugely reassuring.

October

NOVEMBER

Afraid Of Knowledge

So many religions
So many billionaires
So many governments
So many corporations

Watch them fighting
To prevent people
From learning how
Their bodies work

See them giving
Untold fortunes
To ensure nothing
Will ever change

Notice them working
Hard at deadlocking
And doing nothing
Just as they are paid to do

Watch them spending
Millions to keep us
From knowing what's in
The foods we're eating

All four are afraid
Afraid of knowledge
Because knowledge is power
And power is something
Only they should have

November 5, 2016
Portland, Oregon

It's funny how over $20 million of out-of-state money flowed into Oregon to fight against the labeling of genetically modified food.

What are they trying to keep us from finding out?

Flips The Weather Switch

Sunny!
Dry!
Beautiful!
For months on end

(flips the weather switch)

Gloomy!
Rainy!
Soggy!
For months on end

November 5, 2014
Portland, Oregon

This is how it is here.

Dare I Err

Dare I err
On the soft side of compassion?
Should I risk
Putting my heart so far out there?
Is it news
That I'm watching my dreams extinguish?
Is the sun
The one prodding me to feel the view?

November 5, 2014
Portland, Oregon

I'll never know.

As a side note, I did this one in a looping, rhyming fashion that seemed interesting to me based on the first two lines. I would have continued, but it took me a surprisingly long time to come up with this.

Feeling The View

On-mountain
Looking out
Off-mountain
Looking up,
Either way
Living free from demands
And feeling the view
Is the only obligation

> November 5, 2014
> Portland, Oregon

Tabor or Hood, take your pick.

I used a variation of this title in the last poem, "Dare I Err," but I wanted it to be used like I did in this poem. So, now you get two that kind of off-shoot from one another.

The Gurnding Grunkle

The gurnding grunkle of dirty gravel
Grinding, crunching, underfoot
Making more noise in a
Sickening fashion than
Walking across
Something so gross and
Reviling that it is
Preferable I stop here
Leaving the thoughts
Better left undescribed

November 15, 2015
Portland, Oregon

Walking across wet gritty dirt sounds gross when you really listen
to it.

Viscous Anger

Thickly driving
Intently swerving
Hateredly panging
Focusedly reaching
Nightmareously dark
Deliberately inciting
Viscous anger
Reaching, hooking
The undercurrent of discontent
Infectiously breeding
In the profanity-laced moat
Surrounding their self-locked cells
In the decomposing castle
Of their own design
Their own enjoyment
And their own imprisonment

November 15, 2014
Portland, Oregon

Last week I went to see a local Iron Maiden cover band. I like Iron Maiden a lot; always have. Subject matter aside, I find their music to be both beautifully melodic and wonderful fuel for writing action scenes in my books. The opening band was named Chemical Rage and did a set that was so deeply steeped in negative nonsense that I almost left. I forced myself to stay and viewed it as an opportunity to observe a section of life that I normally don't expose myself to. Interesting, but not worth repeating.

Confidence

Confidence
Is infectious
Is awe-inspiring
In the correct amounts
It can accomplish
It can conquer
Anything.
Anything at all.

Confidence
Is repulsing
Is deadening
In the wrong amounts
It can hinder
It can destroy
Everything.
Everything you know.

November 15, 2014
Portland, Oregon

The song "Local God" by Everclear came on my iTunes, and I was instantly inspired to write this.

The Last Rose

Autumn's genocide has swept through
Rusting green and creating carpeting
On every inch of the leafy decoupaged ground
But today
When I looked up, ever so slightly,
I spied the lone holdout from the life-time
The last rose, exploding in full bloom,
Shining like a supernova of life
With twin middle fingers upright
Defiantly in the face of the calendar
Currently pushing Thanksgiving
All the while redefining hardy
As I felt compelled to take a photo
And write a poem in tribute
To Portland's final and lasting rose

November 22, 2014
Portland, Oregon

While walking the dogs about an hour ago, I saw a withered rose bush with one brilliant holdout, shining bright red. If I had seen it a few months ago, surrounded by dozens of contemporaries, it would have been no big deal. This time, however, seeing something not just living, but *thriving* well past autumn's scythe cut through for the year, well, it was very impressive.

Polarized The Remnants

Privacy implies
The secrets within
Will be kept that way
But most want otherwise:
For all to be revealed
So you must choose
Transparency or
Unrepentant exhibitionism
Lately there is no middle ground
So strut your stuff
Or shut it up.
Showing or hiding.
One or the other.
No room for in-between
As modern culture
Has kindly killed that
Preferable option
And polarized the remnants
Leaving a screaming mess
Comprised solely of extremes

November 22, 2014
Portland, Oregon

One or the other with no in-between. These days it's like the greatest sin is to be open-minded.

Bonsai

Double blade of contrasting emotions
Happiness at seeing parents ten years younger
Enjoying a cultural slice of Americana
Sadness at seeing this something
I will never get to taste on my own
As my family tree is like a bonsai
Well-pruned and blooming brightly
But soon with no one to take my place
As the untold hours put into everything
Are sold to strangers at my estate sale
For pennies to the hour
Because no one knows
Nor are they interested

November 22, 2014
Portland, Oregon

Two big things smashed into a small poem with a Large Hadron Collider: First, a scene I saw last fall where a much younger couple with a small kid walked past on their way to Halloween event, all dressed up and happy in the moment. It hit me hard that I'm a decade past that with no children of my own. Second, two months ago we came across an estate sale at a fancy home in the West Hills of Portland. The women was a champion rose grower and won countless awards for her roses over the decades. We picked up half a dozen of her professionally printed planter signs for her various rose varieties. They included names like, "Gratitude," "X-Rated," and "Denver Sunset." The signs were neat, but they served a real purpose for this woman, but nothing for her heirs. This poem is a weird formless mish-mashing of the two unconnected thoughts.

The Wrong Side Of The River

Her whole life rooted to one side
Of the river
Submerged in harsh reality
Steeped in putrid drudgery
Misted in commonplace life
Where creativity and magic
Are not allowed to thrive
When instead
She should have been over here
Where the momentous moments
That inspire are an everyday thing
Where magic abounds all around
And creativity flows from the taps
She has a chance
If she allows herself
To change perspective
To change location
And choose really living
Over merely existing
On the wrong side of the river

November 22, 2014
Portland, Oregon

Vancouver, Washington versus Portland, Oregon. There is no contest as this match was decided by a knockout even before the contestants entered the ring.

The Alarm

The final glance
The last breath
Isn't a limiting thing
Isn't anything to be feared
But merely the alarm
Ringing, ringing, ringing
And awakening you
In the in-between place
Where reliving,
Relaxing, and planning
Take place in perfect
Amounts and harmony
Before the big dive,
Head-first, back into it,
The next incarnation,
Where you try a new part
In a brand-new you
In the play we all play
For eternal ever after

November, 27, 2014
Portland, Oregon

There is a part of me that naturally wants to dissuade myself from writing about the spiritual and what I know to be true. The rest of me doesn't care much for being stifled.

Awakening

The person who questions
What came before
Is awakening
From a generational sleep
The confines of which
Were imposed by
Prior elders whose names
Are completely lost to you.
Ways of thinking
Ways of life
All of which have no bearing
Upon you here and now
None of which actually defines
How you really feel
Today, in this moment.
So why continue to adhere
To a philosophy for no other reason
Than your ignorant predecessors
Did this to explain the world
Before its secrets were known
And exposed by science?
Don't.
Instead, awake and feel the world
According to your own dictates
Live the best life you can imagine
Free from oppression
Away from negativity
Doing just what feels right
And nothing else

                    November 27, 2014
                    Portland, Oregon

I honestly didn't mean to follow up a poem called "The Alarm"
with one called "Awakening" but I guess it kinda sorta happened.
With this, I was thinking about a co-worker who holds closely to

his religious faith and has been expressing questions and thoughts about spirituality, which seems to indicate that he is growing and reaching beyond the limited confines of his religion. I pointed him in the way I knew based on the brief time allowed by our lunch break.

I think it was enough because he wrote to me on his day off asking for more.

Onion Dip Or Mashed Potatoes

This afternoon
When responding to
A snack attack situation
I reached into the fridge
Based on the intelligence
There was dip to be had
And pulled out a glass bowl,
Grabbed the bag of chips,
And promptly couched it.
After popping off the lid
I was a little confused
Because I didn't know if this was
Onion dip or mashed potatoes
It was thick like potatoes
And had bits of onion fleck-things
But it smelled like strong garlic
I grabbed a test chip, scooped, and bit
Um…well…I really couldn't tell
Maybe the temperature was too low
And it firmed up in a weird way
I really don't know.
Second scoop and bite
Didn't give me any more info
So I followed it up with more
This was getting distressing
Onion dip or mashed potatoes
Several chips in I still don't know
The flavor was fine
But the consistency was all wrong
Like a Crystal Pepsi
When you want a Dr. Pepper
The wrongness of this situation
Grew with each passing bite
Until I shut the bag
And quit the dip.

Two days later,

I still don't know
What I was eating
Nor is it something
I want to think about again.

November 29, 2014
Portland, Oregon

This seriously happened. Kari said she made French onion dip (yay!). When I got the chips and the bowl of dip, something didn't look right. I didn't let it stop me but, wow, it just didn't seem right. After about 10 minutes I put it back, still not knowing what I ate.

Update: I'm pretty sure it was, in fact, French onion dip. Kari had added extra stuff to it like fresh minced garlic and put it in the fridge for a few days. My guess is that the fridge might have been a touch cold, causing it to fuse together into something that resembled mashed potatoes.

Clicking The Keyboard

Clicking the keyboard
At just the right moment
Causing a spark
Bursting, crackling, upward
Into my mind
Hitting a vein
Diving, speeding, deep
Into myself
Connecting the two selves
In just the right way
Freeing myself to create

November 29, 2014
Portland, Oregon

This was me the other night. Everything seemed to click just right and my fingers flew across the keyboard imparting creativity directly to the screen.

Thanksgiving/Thankstaking

The dichotomy of our culture
Expressed fully and completely
Within one hypocritical day:

Thanksgiving

Where we travel far and wide
And gather together as family
To celebrate and express
How thankful we truly are

Bellies full to the point of
Bursting with gluttony
We recline and rest up
For the battle ahead:

Thankstaking

Strategy ready, flyers in-hand
The doors open and we surge
A rush and a push and the TV is ours
Knocked over a dozen others
In the process but that's ok,
We got what we came for
And that's what's important
To be thankful for what we have

November 29, 2014
Portland, Oregon

Mass consumerism is a disease and the box stores on Thanksgiving
and Black Friday are the petri dishes where this insidious side of
Americana gets cultivated and is allowed (and encouraged!) to
thrive in its disgusting mob-mentality way year after year. It

sickens me to see the videos where people are trampled or are fighting over some useless piece of junk they don't really need.

A Glance With Meaning

A glance
With meaning
Can weigh more
Can cause hearts
To skip beats
A million times more
Can actually change lives
More than soulless fucking
Could or would ever do
Because when the act
Is backed up with nothing
Nothing is what you're left with

November 29, 2014
Portland, Oregon

Empty Walls

Walking past an apartment
With no curtains, freely
Allowing my eyes in for a visit
I look past the three people
Drinking Rainier canned beer
To the empty walls behind them
And I wonder if that's the cause
Of some people's empty lives
Where they have nothing but
Blank walls staring back at them
Every hour of every day
No art, no inspiration, no nothing
Do empty walls equal empty lives?
I don't know, but it certainty
Cannot be enriching or uplifting
In any reasonable way

November 29, 2014
Portland, Oregon

This evening I went for a short walk (it was cold) down to Hawthorne when I couldn't help but to stare inside the large window of this one crappy-looking apartment. There were three (or four) people sitting around drinking canned beer (I fictionalized it a bit and said they were drinking the Pacific Northwest's go-to low-budget beer: Rainier) but my eyes couldn't help but to focus not on the people, but on the walls of their apartment; they were empty. Nothing. No art. No pictures. No nothing. It was weird. I spent the rest of my walk wondering what kind of person doesn't hang up anything on their walls, and then wondering what kind of life would it be like to not want something inspirational around to look at.

This very brief glimpse of a stranger's apartment on my walk, combined with listening to Lambchop's "Sharing A Gibson With Martin Luther King Jr." (from *Live At XX Merge*) fueled the writing of this poem.

November

The Taborist

DECEMBER

Searching for the 31st

At work, or rather, at the bank
Delivering cash deposits
Reviewing the receipts
Handed back to me
When I notice there's a day missing
28, 29, 30, 1, 2
Where's the 31st?
I go through the slips
One at a time, carefully twisting
Each one, individually to make sure
One day didn't slip on by
No luck
I asked the teller if, by chance,
I didn't get a receipt
She checked and said no
I drove back to work and
Dove onto my desk
Searching for the 31st
For the cash deposit
But discovered that the entire day
Was completely gone
Not just the deposit, but all paperwork
Everything
Vanished
Goddamn.
After tearing through
Everything five more times
I opened my email to ask
(demand)
The co-worker who did the deposits
Where the missing day was
Two sentences in, I stop,
Pick up my phone, and start a text
Just so I can get a more immediate response
Two sentences in, I stop,
Look up at the calendar, and stare
28, 29, 30, 1, 2

December

Last month was November
Instantly explaining the day away
And making me feel like quite the heel

I deleted my text, closed my email
And laughed to myself

> December 3, 2014
> Vancouver, Washington

I'm normally very good with dates but wow, this one had me going for an unusually long time.

From The Stranger You

Ten years today
I awoke to an email
From the stranger you
That changed my life
Dinner lead to drinks
Drinks lead to the Atlantic
For a December ocean-touch
Things sped up from there
And before we knew it
We were living together,
In Paris, engaged, moved away,
Moved again, perfectly married,
And moved many more times
Over the flurry of calendar pages
Until we find ourselves
Right here on this day
A decade after the email
That brought us together
Countless miles traveled
With one another
Lives sorted out, dreams actualized,
The big things, the little things,
All known, all answered, all set,
All done in a decade
Which makes me light up inside
Wondering what's in store
For our next ten years

December 4, 2014
Portland, Oregon

Happy ten years! I love you!

The Kinetic Crew

The kinetic crew
Flowing energetic
Every time they meet
Ideas spreading
Inspiration sparking
From one to another
Lifting all to a higher
Place, increasing their
View, changing their
Perspective, enlightening
And circling around again
To repeat the process
To further enrich their lives

December 5, 2014
Portland, Oregon

My wife is part of a "Mastermind Group" of women who meet up every few weeks to talk about their businesses and life in general. Tonight it's being hosted at our house. I'm not quite invited to their meeting, but it's interesting to be sitting here in the office, half listening to them and feeling their positive energy billowing about.

It's neat.

Tabor Rainbow

While standing at the sink
Waiting for the water to warm
I looked up and saw the blast of color
The sharply-defined Tabor rainbow
Boldly arcing before the dark gray
Over the neighbor's house
And planting, firmly, on the slope
I'm guessing illuminating the ideal spot
Where one could have a great view
Of the ice-packed Mount Saint Helens
And the airy space where its peak
Used to be.
Or…maybe not.
I dunno.
It's probably highlighting a magical nut
To a down-on-its-luck squirrel for all I know
Anyway, hey, cool rainbow.

December 5, 2014
Portland, Oregon

I saw this the other day and was impressed with it so I started
writing. When I came back to this poem tonight, I was clearly in a
very different place and not afraid to steer it in a weirdly
unexpected direction.

Innocent

The power is clearly too heavy
For those choosing to wield it
With each swing of their "justice"
It's claiming lives of the innocent

December 5, 2014
Portland, Oregon

Too many innocent people are dying because those who should be protecting the population are, instead, too afraid so they are placing their instinctive trust in deadly force instead of relying on their abilities and training.

Where Your Past Sleeps Soundly

You'll never have a future in the bed
Where your past sleeps soundly
Staying and acquiescing permanently
Forever always wondering what
Your alternate future had in store
Without experiencing anything new
Or, instead, making a different decision:
To move beyond and live life boldly
Choosing a new path filled with wonder
And a million unconsidered things
Each and every one uplifting and increasing
Your awareness of what life could hold
And provide for the awesomeness of you
If only you dared to dream,
Believe, and make it happen

December 5, 2014
Portland, Oregon

Disassociate yourself with your past and choose to live right now.

The Next Day

When the adrenaline has dried up
Like the love left behind
When the smell of the moment
Has dissipated into blandness
When the fires of connectivity
Resemble bitter cold ashes
When your fondest memories
Are looping in your head
When the screams of intensity
Are replaced with normalcy
Is how you know you've crossed
From the frameable moments,
Perfection with each blink,
To the drudgery of the next day
Steeped in the commonality
Where you return to repetition

December 5, 2014
Portland, Oregon

Moments enjoyed and lost.

Cross-Contamination

Piñon wood aroma
From a nearby fireplace
Hauntingly beautiful
Lifting me into the air
With every single step
With every single breath
I pull in the rich beauty
And…something's wrong
Dryer and fabric softener.
Oh, no, no, no!
My moment of perfection
Is being usurped and ruined
By cross-contamination
From another's dryer vent
The mix of aromas
The highs of piñon
The lows of Snuggle
With me frowning
Stuck in the middle

December 6, 2014
Portland, Oregon

Tonight Kari went to the Sapphire Hotel on Hawthorne with a
friend. I was to meet them later to walk Kari home. On the way
down, I walked past a house that was burning piñon wood in their
fireplace and it smelled amazing.

Wow!

On our way back home, I kept telling her about this house and how
great it was. When we approached, it smelled just as good as I had
foretold. Then, without warning, we got a large whiff of dryer
fabric softener sheets that completely ruined the moment.

I'm sure there are worse things we could have smelled at that moment, but it's hard to go from something so wonderful to something so not-wonderful so quickly.

Porch Party

Your neighbor throwing a porch party
Is no big deal when you live
In the remoteness of rural Vermont
But when you're in Portland, Oregon
And your house is less than eight feet
From the cacophonic din
Of the talkers within
From the thumping bass
And the beer bottle's clink
The waves of laughter
And general noise
Associated with a porch party
Well, in that case, it's not so great

December 6, 2014
Portland, Oregon

Since these neighbors moved in this past summer, they've had three or four big parties. Not just normal gatherings of friends, but the kind of get-together where twenty or thirty people show up. They're actually pretty low-key, but there's a lot of them and I can hear their concentrated talking above the music I'm playing on my computer right now.

The most interesting aspect about their parties is the general makeup of the people who attend. "Try-Hard Hipsters" make up just about 80% of their party attendees. When I say, "Try-Hard Hipsters" I mean the type of men who have beards, years in the making, or moustaches wearing more wax than most floors. Too-small hats, odd vintage bikes galore, and monocles. I would not be surprised if two or three people over there were carrying original 1980s Trapper Keepers. Why? Just because that's what hipsters do. (NOTE: this paragraph may contain inflated exaggeration.)

For their second party, they invited us over, but we never went. I dunno why. We were home at the time, but I think we just didn't feel like doing anything social. They have not invited us over since.

I wonder if it has to do with how much our dogs like to pee on their bottom step?

No, I'm pretty sure they've never seen that happen.

Hm.

Actually, never mind. I'm probably just jealous since I don't have enough friends to fill a couch, much less an entire house.

Creativity

Whenever I want it,
Whenever I reach for it,
Without fail, it's there:
The creativity I have been blessed with
Hand in my pocket
I pull it out and find
A word, a phrase, a poem,
Something neat and interesting
Something I can use later;
My sixth sense kicks in
And my attention is pulled
To a specific point just in time
To be witness to a unique thing
So I pull out my phone
Take a photo or jot a note
Something to record what I saw.
I need to experience the magic of life
And this amazing Universe
Can't help but accommodate
Each and every time
A request goes out
From me to out there
Even if I'm not aware of it
Which is why
Every day
In every way
I am thankful
For the energy
And the responsiveness
I have experienced
With this life

December 6, 2014
Portland, Oregon

I've heard people talk about "writer's block," but it's something I've never experienced. Honestly, and I'm not being a braggy braggart when I say this, I don't think I could ever be sidelined with writer's block. Whenever I need the creative push, it's there. Whenever I need to experience something new and interesting, oh, hey, look at this, here's what I was looking for. If I had more time and more energy, I could whip out novels like a champ.

Until then, I'll continue writing poetry like a champ.

Betelgeusing Toward Tabor

The big winter sky man
The imposing astral feature
Everyone can quickly find
Is up there, doing his thing
With his inflamed shoulder
Betelgeusing toward Tabor
While being swept away
As his feet skid through
Nearby stellar debris
Trying with all his might
To return to Mount Tabor
Until the twin weapons,
The horizon and the sun,
Work in tandem with time,
To vanquish Orion for the night

December 20, 2014
Portland, Oregon

The other night I happened to see an actual cloudless, clear night and, BOOM, there he was: Orion. He was tilted and facing the top of Mount Tabor as if he was trying hard to return to the small tree-topped extinct volcano core, but the rotation of the Earth had other plans and instead pulled him away, across the sky, Westward.

It was interesting to think of how this "eternal figure" in the sky was undergoing a secret battle each and every night above our heads and no one knew.

What's going to happen in a few million years when Betelgeuse goes supernova? I think it'll cause Orion a very big headache. Or, at the very least set his shoulder and arm area ablaze. Maybe then it won't even look like a person, but something like a sombrero sitting atop a belt. Maybe it would be known as "The Accessory Constellation" or "Orion's Closet."

I think I really like that one. "Orion's Closet." Maybe they can figure out other things like socks and a hat or something from the stars around him.

Clumsy Superhero

She's a small-town hero
Who doesn't wear a cape
One hundred eighty years old
But only looks seventeen
Invincible and eternal
Is just one of many
Powers (or curses) she carries

As the decades wore on
She noticed her mis-steps
Stumbled off a building here
Run over by a train there
The frequency of these
Hung heavy in her mind
As she wondered to herself
Am I trying to do myself in?

After weeks of thought
And a few more accidents
She came to the conclusion
The fresh-faced honesty
That yes, she was curious
About death, that elusive bitch,
Who had no problem claiming
Everyone she ever knew and loved
But seemed completely unaware
Of her presence, of her continued
Existence in this painful plane;

That yes, she had wondered
What it would actually take
To finally finish things here
To finally be free of life
And venture on to the unknown
That has been so secretly
So tightly kept from her;

But life is more complex
Than wishes can express
And as that train slammed her
And her body is flung away
Mid-air movement captivated:
A sparrow bobbing in flight
Her eyes appreciated
The perfection of nature
Every glimpse
Every movement
Every little everything
Made her crave more
Of life and the energy
That comprises all of it;
Lying in the grass
By the oily tracks
Bruised, battered, in pain,
But completely alive
And healing quickly,
That olden-day saying
Her brother used to say
Rang out loud in her mind:
Everything happens for a reason.
While she didn't know
What purpose it served
To make her immortal
She thought that, for the time being,
Things were better left
This way, as it really was,
And to continue down
The way, the path,
The Universe
Had chosen for her
Because there was a reason
And she was determined
To find the one reply
Answering her lifetimes
Of asking, "Why?"

December 21, 2014
Portland, Oregon

I got to thinking today about Emily Dickinson, Superhero and how she would be dealing with her powers if she was still alive today. The powers, she'd be used to, no problem. I think she'd be still grappling with the whole immortality thing which got me wondering if she would sit and think about it, or be slightly clumsy…sorta on purpose.

Defeated And Reheated

In this city full of atheists
And those who are confident
With their spiritual awareness
You'd think there'd be more
In the form of places and choices
Of restaurants open on Christmas
But apart from the Doug Fir Lounge,
Overflowing with a line out the door,
We only saw a couple of Thai places
So we did the only logical thing:
We returned home, defeated
And reheated some leftovers

December 25, 2014
Portland, Oregon

Seriously, you'd think that (*especially*) in this city you'd be able to find some good restaurants open on Christmas but, sadly, it was not the case.

Between November And Now

Back a month, lights landed
Everywhere my arms stretched
The tree went up before Thanksgiving
The decorations soon followed
Seasonal music played lightly
Filling the house with gentle cheer
But something since happened
The reason for the season
Vanished somewhere between
November and now

I don't know where it went
The trappings were all there
The music still played
The lights flickered every night

All I know is the primary day
Of this entire holiday season
Ceased to be important
As if the feelings stopped
While the empty commercialism
Still bore on, all around me
Drilling deeply for dollars
In the always fertile holy ground
That religion provides us

December 25, 2014
Portland, Oregon

In November, I was playing Christmas music a week or two before
Thanksgiving. Then, in mid-December…nothing. It's like the
Christmas spirit just vanished and the day became just like any
other.

Like Cordwood

The bad taste that lingers and stays
Is the one the memory forms around
And, like cordwood, begins to stack
Small and easily missable at first
As the years pass, it can only grow
Until your storage shed is overfull
And you're left with two choices:
Expand the shed and keep stacking,
Or burn it down and never stack again.

December 27, 2014
Portland, Oregon

I feel like this one should have been a lot longer, but this is where I'm stopping.

Sidestepping Crow

Walking the dogs on my street
Drizzly late Sunday morning
When one starts to speed up
I see his intentions directed
At a simple crow, standing
There on the sidewalk,
And as we approached
It walked in a circuitous path
Out into the street, keeping us
Away from it at the same distance
The dogs lost interest but I didn't
As the sidestepping crow and I
Watched each other until it passed
Back onto the sidewalk behind us
And we all resumed our day

December 28, 2014
Portland, Oregon

Energy

Every atom in your body is billions of years old.
Founded in the explosive forge of a dying star
Recycled, reused, and recombined
Thousands of time since then
Until everything came together just right
Making the physical you
Imagine, for a moment (or a lifetime),
What the spiritual you is comprised of
An energy more everlasting
Than our paltry conception of time
Something more powerful
Than the stars in the night sky
The mysteriousness of it allowing us to
Slip past the grip of death
And go to the perfect place
Between each round of life

> December 28, 2014
> Portland, Oregon

Before Handwriting Fell

Thinking back to the days
Before handwriting fell
Hard and fast into disuse
out of favor and practice
I would write untold letters,
Go to the post office to send
The physical communication
I would enjoy opening
My mailbox, a letter there,
Sit and spend real time
Seeing, reading, smelling,
The paper, the words,
The whole experience,
And I knew where my
Stamps and envelopes were
Seems so archaic and quaint
Compared to modern days
Where ease and speed
Are what matters most
From the 90s to today
As the keyboard, trim
And slimmed down,
Plugged itself into power
And captured us all

December 28, 2014
Portland, Oregon

This one had been sitting in Line Ideas for about two years, so I
dusted it off and gave it life.

A Field Day

Once I found myself
Talking about books
With a non-reader.
Soon, it became clear to me
He didn't know the difference
Between fiction and non-fiction.
When I told him I wrote sci-fi
He replied, "With all the stuff
About archeology these days,
You should have a field day!"
Yes, sir. A field day, indeed.

December 28, 2014
Portland, Oregon

This had been sitting in Line Ideas for at least three years, maybe more. Short and weird, but true.

Every Second

Every second
Is questioned
Every motive
Is scrutinized
Every action
Must be explained
Every thing done
Must be answered for
The lasting of this
Cannot be for long
As patience dries out
And unquestionably brittles
Under taut knuckles

December 28, 2014
Portland, Oregon

Looking Back On This Year

Looking back on this year
Some good things happened
So did some not great things
I got settled into my new city
I got back into my old career
My creative output dwindled
To nearly nothing
Books in progress
Lay neglected save for perusals
And the minutest of changes
I am glad the end of the year
Nicely coincides with right now
Because I'm getting it together
And I'll be starting the year 2015
Off right from the very get-go
Blasting off and not looking back

>   December 28, 2014
>   Portland, Oregon

Get. It. Done.

The Taborist

ACKNOWLEDGEMENTS

I would like to thank the following people for their help and support:

Kari Chapin, my wife, who is awesome and continues to actively encourage this writing thing I do.

My family: Sharon Jandrow, Todd Nixon, Ron and Robyn Chapin, and Janis McWayne who have given a lot of help and support while I wrote.

Finally, *YOU!* I am still always wow, wow, wowed with amazement when people set aside hours of their time to read my writings. Seriously, thank you. It means a whole lot to me.

IF YOU ENJOYED THIS COLLECTION
Please consider rating it at Amazon.com. As an independent author, having people review my works is critical in helping to increase my exposure and letting new people discover books like this. Thank you!

OTHER BOOKS WRITTEN BY ERIC NIXON
Anything But Dreams: A Poetry Collection
Lost In Thought: A Poetry Collection
Emily Dickinson, Superhero – Vol.1
Trying Not To Blink: 2012 Poetry Collection
The Entire Universe: 2013 Poetry Collection

FIND ERIC NIXON ONLINE
Website: EricNixon.net
Website: EmilyDickinsonSuperhero.com
Instagram: @EricNixon
Twitter: @EricNixon
Twitter: @EmilyDSuperhero
Pinterest: EmilyDSuperhero
My poem, "Riding The Red Line" at The Writer's Almanac:
http://writersalmanac.publicradio.org/index.php?date=2011/08/29

www.ingramcontent.com/pod-product-compliance
Lightning Source LLC
Chambersburg PA
CBHW061824040426
42447CB00012B/2808